HARNESSING ENERGY · HARNESSING ENERGY

SOLAR POWER

BY DIANE BAILEY

HARNESSING ENERGY

HARNESSING ENERGY

TABLE OF CONTENTS

PEACE AND WAR. WEALTH AND POVERTY. PROGRESS AND SETBACKS. HISTORY HAS BROUGHT HUGE SWINGS IN THE HUMAN CONDITION, AND WITH EVERY CHOICE PEOPLE MAKE, THERE IS THE POTENTIAL TO MOVE FORWARD OR STEP BACKWARD. AT THE CORE OF THIS CONTINUAL STRUGGLE HAS BEEN THE QUEST FOR ENERGY. ENERGY GAVE HUMANS POWER AND MOTIVATED THEM TO DO GREAT THINGS—WITH BOTH POSITIVE AND NEGATIVE EFFECTS. WITHOUT ENERGY, PEOPLE WOULD NOT BE ABLE TO DRIVE CARS, OPERATE COMPUTERS, OR POWER FACTORIES. WARS ARE FOUGHT TRYING TO DOMINATE SOURCES OF ENERGY. FORTUNES ARE MADE AND LOST DEPENDING ON HOW THAT ENERGY IS MANAGED. THE LAWS OF PHYSICS STATE THAT ENERGY CANNOT BE CREATED OR DESTROYED. THAT IS TRUE, BUT ENERGY CAN BE HARNESSED AND DIRECTED. IT CAN BE WASTED, OR IT CAN BE COAXED INTO EFFICIENCY. CIVILIZATIONS AND TECHNOLOGIES HAVE LEAPED FORWARD—AND SOMETIMES BACKWARD—AS HUMANS HAVE TAPPED INTO EARTH'S SOURCES OF ENERGY.

*Solar technology allows humans
to tap into the sun's energy.*

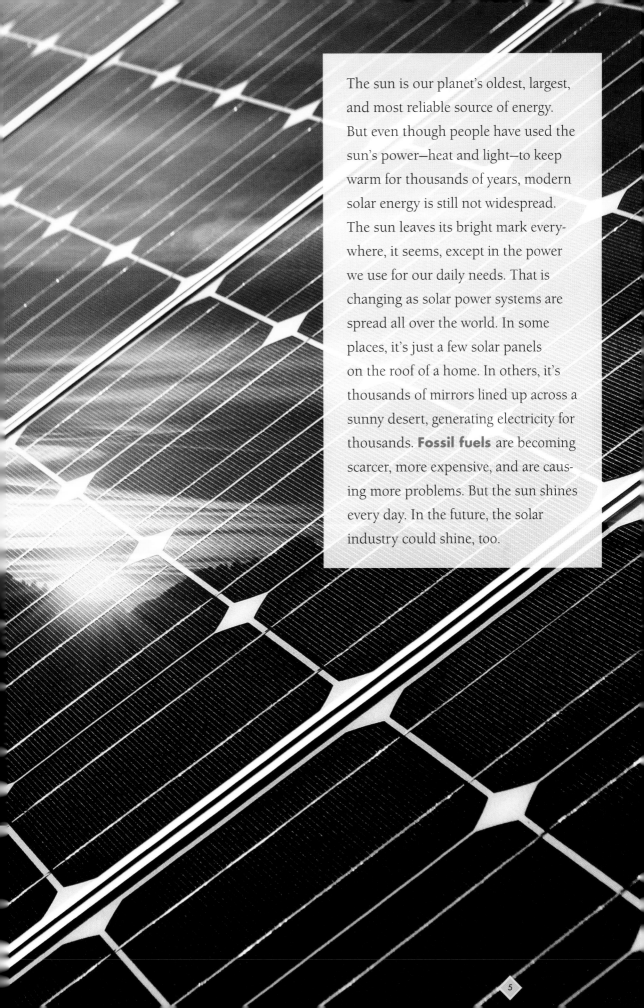

The sun is our planet's oldest, largest, and most reliable source of energy. But even though people have used the sun's power—heat and light—to keep warm for thousands of years, modern solar energy is still not widespread. The sun leaves its bright mark every-where, it seems, except in the power we use for our daily needs. That is changing as solar power systems are spread all over the world. In some places, it's just a few solar panels on the roof of a home. In others, it's thousands of mirrors lined up across a sunny desert, generating electricity for thousands. **Fossil fuels** are becoming scarcer, more expensive, and are caus-ing more problems. But the sun shines every day. In the future, the solar industry could shine, too.

CHAPTER ONE

NOTHING NEW UNDER THE SUN

THE SUN IS THE ULTIMATE SERVANT. It doesn't argue, never takes a day off, and even works for free. Ancient peoples recognized that the sun, just like a hard-working servant, provided everything in their lives. Its heat gave them warmth. Food came from plants nourished by sunshine. Grateful for its power and energy, many cultures worshiped the sun, viewing it as a **deity**. Today, people are less likely to worship the sun, but it's still the source of virtually all Earth's energy. Although 93 million miles (150 million km) away, this is one long-distance relationship that's not going to fizzle out.

Ancient Egyptians thought of the sun as a great boat that carried the gods across the sky.

People can save money and make use of passive solar energy for drying clothes or heating buildings.

Each second, the sun burns up millions of tons of its own mass, turning it into light and heat. Only a tiny fraction of that energy ever reaches Earth. Even so, in less than an hour and a half, the sun delivers enough energy to power the world's people for an entire year! It's estimated that just 20 days of sunlight provide as much energy as is stored in all the world's reserves of fossil fuels. Of course, people can capture only a very small portion of all that solar energy, but fortunately, that's all they need.

At its most basic level, solar energy is easy to use. All it requires is the sun and something that absorbs heat. Drying clothes outside uses solar energy. So does frying an egg on the sidewalk on a hot summer day. (Make sure it's a clean sidewalk first.) This passive solar energy is simply heat and light that is collected from the sun. It does not involve converting the sun's energy into another form, such as electricity, as active solar technology does. People have used passive solar energy for thousands of years. In ancient Greece and Rome, architects and engineers designed towns and cities to have as many homes as possible facing south, where they could get the most sun in the winter. As cities grew, more buildings sometimes blocked the sun from reaching existing structures. In the sixth century A.D., the Romans passed a law making it illegal to construct a building

In a greenhouse, warm air rises through a process called convection and is trapped by the walls and roof.

that would prevent sunlight from reaching the buildings around it. The people had a right to light. Later, people discovered the power of glass to trap heat. They put windows in their houses and constructed greenhouses to grow plants, even when it was cold outside. Solar power was also used to heat water. Water tanks were painted black, since black absorbs more heat than other colors. The warm water was used for cooking, washing clothes and dishes, and bathing.

In one story, from the third century B.C., the Greek mathematician and scientist Archimedes told soldiers to direct their bronze shields toward the sun, and then mirror them at enemy Roman ships, making them catch fire. It's the same basic principle as using a magnifying glass to focus sunlight on a dry leaf, heating the leaf until it ignites. This incident is probably more legend than truth, but it shows that people recognized that the sun's power could also be concentrated. Today, concentrated solar power (CSP), using the same fundamental methods of focused sunlight, is applied in commercial solar power plants.

Getting more power out of the sun is a goal for the modern solar industry. Direct solar heat is helpful, but it's not enough to meet the power needs of today's societies.

Wind can supplement solar power, providing after-dark energy.

People want hot showers, but solar-heated water is often just "warm." Solar-heated houses are warmer than the outdoors, but that's not always enough during a cold winter. People also want enough energy to run appliances such as refrigerators, televisions, and computers. Much of this power comes from electricity, an extremely versatile means of delivering energy.

The main challenge for solar power today is converting it into electricity. This is accomplished in either of two ways. One is concentrated solar power. This captures the sun's heat energy. The heat is collected and then used to make steam. The pressure of the steam spins the blades of a **turbine**, which in turn powers a magnet that generates electricity. Another solar technology is photovoltaics. This word is a combination of two words. *Photo* means "light" in Greek, and *voltaic* refers to electricity. In a photovoltaic (PV) system, the sun's light is converted directly into electricity when it interacts with certain elements.

Horace Bénédict de Saussure developed the electrometer to measure energy potential.

By the 1700s and 1800s, scientists were conducting experiments with solar power. The results of those experiments form the basis of today's industry. In 1767, the Swiss naturalist Horace Bénédict de Saussure made the first solar oven, a box with glass panels that could reach about 230 °F (110 °C). While some scientists continued experimenting with the sun's thermal powers, in 1839, French scientist Alexandre-Edmond Becquerel observed the photovoltaic effect. It was a completely different way that the sun could produce energy. Nearly 50 years later, in 1883, American inventor Charles Fritts built an operational working photovoltaic solar cell, using the element selenium. However, his cell converted only about 1 percent of the sun's energy into electricity.

Solar cell development continued in the first half of the 20th century, using selenium as Fritts had, but the problem of effectiveness remained. Then researchers at Bell Labs in the United States accidentally discovered that another element, silicon, was even better at converting light to electricity. Real progress started to happen. In 1954, the Bell researchers displayed the world's first practical solar cell, using it to run a transistor radio. The news media latched onto the success. A 1957 *BusinessWeek* article speculated about a solar future. The possibilities included a car that was automatically steered by solar power, enabling its passengers to have fun. The article noted, "All the riders could sit comfortably in the back seat and perhaps watch solar-powered TV." These predictions ended up being a bit too optimistic. Solar power was expensive, but fossil fuels were cheap. Some ideal uses for solar were apparent—such as in the space program—but solar energy for daily use faded into the background.

Solar made a comeback in the 1970s. In 1973, oil suppliers in the Middle East hiked up their prices, causing shortages everywhere. Countries the world over started scrambling to find new sources of energy. U.S. president Jimmy Carter, elected in 1976, approved $3 billion in funding for solar research. In 1979, he held a press conference on the roof of the White House, where solar panels were being installed. It symbolized a new era of energy for the U.S. "No one can ever embargo the sun," Carter said.

However, after the oil crisis passed, prices came back down. **Renewable** energy didn't seem as important. The next president, Ronald Reagan, cut solar funding and took the roof panels down. At the time, the U.S. was the world leader in solar research. When it put the brakes on research and development, the rest of the world followed suit. Solar entered another dark age throughout the rest of the 1980s and into the 1990s as fossil fuel prices stayed low.

Back in 1931, American inventor Thomas Edison had said, "I'd put my money on the sun and solar energy. What a source of power! I hope we don't have to run out of oil and coal before we tackle that." In a way, Edison got his wish. The world hadn't run out of fossil fuels by the late 1990s, but the cost was creeping up again. Also, scientists were beginning to realize that fossil fuels polluted the environment and contributed to **global warming**. Solar energy was the new kid at school. It hadn't proven itself, but it did show promise. Maybe it could brighten the world's energy future.

Several of the 32 solar panels President Carter installed on the White House roof now reside in museums.

CHAPTER TWO

THE SPREAD OF SOLAR

BY THE 1990S, THE TIME WAS RIGHT AGAIN TO DO THE MATH ON SOLAR ENERGY. Perhaps scientists and government officials pulled out their solar-powered calculators to help them. These devices came from Japan, one of the first countries to embrace solar research after the 1970s oil crisis. In 1995, Japan started a program to put solar panels on 70,000 rooftops across the country. Germany also threw itself into developing solar energy. It followed Japan's lead in 1999, but aimed for 100,000 rooftops.

In Tokyo, Japan, sunlight captured by solar panels above sidewalks is used for electricity and heat.

These countries' commitment to solar power didn't have much to do with the amount of sunlight they got. What they had in common was a lack of fossil fuels. Both felt the need to develop alternative energy sources.

While Japan and Germany got a head start, today, many countries are increasing their solar resources. According to research from the energy company British Petroleum (BP), Germany produces more solar power than any other country. Italy is next, and Japan, the U.S., and Spain aren't far behind. China is also busy adding new plants. In 2011, India's National Solar Mission increased the country's solar power by an astonishing 62 percent. There are also efforts to encourage solar on a smaller scale. For example, South Africa has launched a program to install solar water heaters in a million homes by 2014. Globally, solar has grown faster than any other form of energy in the last decade. Most of that has been in PV systems. In 2005, there were less than five gigawatts of installed PV solar power in the entire world. (A gigawatt can power roughly one million homes.) By 2012, that number was up to about 65 gigawatts.

Germany has built solar collection fields to supplement its energy resources.

Colorado's National Energy Laboratory has developed new technologies for thin-film solar panels.

In a PV system, sunlight strikes a substance, such as silicon, that has been coated with chemicals. The energy from the light disturbs the **electrons** in the silicon **atoms**. They disconnect from the atom and form an electric current. Conventional PV panels are encased in a solid frame. But "thin-film" PV is a flexible material that can be rolled out and applied to a backing, like a sticker. These solar cells are less efficient but more versatile. In addition, thin-film cells don't use silicon. Silicon is not necessarily the best substance for converting sunlight into energy, but it was familiar and available when solar first hit the big time. Now some researchers are trying other materials. Some cells use a mix of several chemical elements. CIGS technology takes its name from the elements it uses: copper, indium, gallium, and selenium. This combination of substances absorbs more light, boosting the overall effectiveness of the cells.

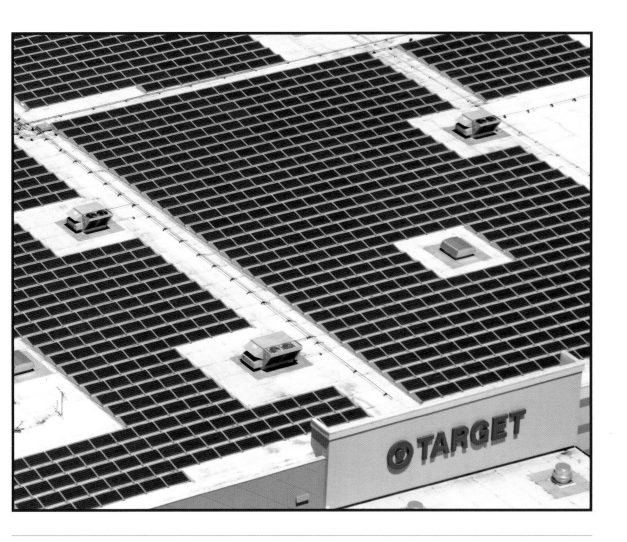

Target outfitted several of its California stores with solar panels as part of a corporate energy plan.

One advantage to PV systems is that they don't need a huge **infrastructure** to work. They are a collection of individual pieces that can operate with a few panels or with hundreds. Large PV power plants can cover acres of land. These plants are designed to provide electricity to a **power grid** that distributes the power to customers. PV can be easily downsized, too. Someone who wants to go solo can install just a few panels on the roof of a home or business. In the U.S., large stores such as Costco, Kohl's, and IKEA are also big customers for PV power. These stores are usually sprawling buildings. It's expensive to keep them at temperatures comfortable enough for shoppers. Collectively, they have many square miles of rooftops available to suck up the sun and use it to power heaters or air conditioners. Solar is a great solution for such places.

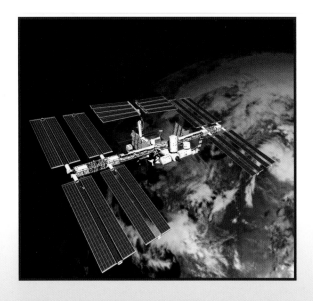

PV solar power can produce electricity on site, without having to be connected to a grid. That makes it ideal for isolated places. It can power emergency call boxes by the side of the freeway, or run lights and appliances in areas that aren't connected to a central power grid. It's also great in space. Solar cells on satellites beam back information used to create maps. They also help run equipment on spacecraft that visit other planets, such as the Mars rovers. Paolo Frankl, the head of the

PV cells on satellites (above) convert light to electricity, while heliostats help CSP plants (below) change light into heat.

renewable energy division of the International Energy Agency (IEA), said in a 2011 interview with Bloomberg News, "The strength of solar is the incredible variety and flexibility of applications, from small scale to big scale."

While photovoltaics have seen the most growth over the last decade, concentrated solar power technology has also made steps forward. CSP systems rely on the sun's heat. Special mirrors, called heliostats, follow the path of the sun and constantly focus its heat.

CSP plants can be constructed in a number of ways. A dish system looks like a large, slightly curved plate. Sunlight is directed onto fluid in an engine, and the expanding liquid pushes a **piston** to run the engine. Typically, the engines are used to generate electricity. Another arrangement for a CSP plant involves the **parabolic** trough system. This looks like a pipe cut in half the long way. The trough is lined with mirrors that focus sunlight on a tube filled with oil. The hot oil is then

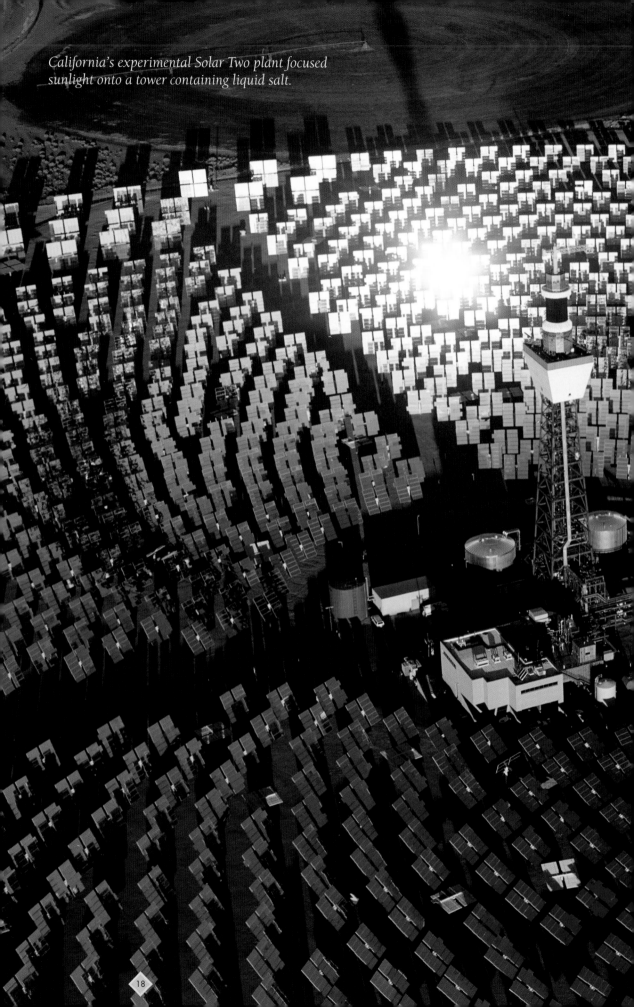

California's experimental Solar Two plant focused sunlight onto a tower containing liquid salt.

used to boil water to produce steam for a generator. A power tower is a third approach. A 300-foot-high (91 m) tower is covered in mirrors that channel sunlight onto a central spot.

Electricity provides instant, constant power to people's homes and businesses. But it has one big technological drawback: it's difficult to store. It's not impossible, but it's expensive. As a result, power plant operators usually decide to "use it or lose it"—but do not save it. That's a problem for solar power, because sunlight is **intermittent**. It's limited or unpredictable on cloudy days and completely absent at night. An ongoing challenge is trying to balance the amount of sun with customers' demand for electricity. When there's no sun, there must be some kind of backup system in place.

A prime advantage to CSP systems is that they have the potential to store energy. One technology involves using solar power to heat **molten** salts. The salts can be heated to a very high temperature, about 1,000 °F (538 °C). They can also hold their heat for several hours, or even days. The stored heat can continue to run a generator, even after the sun has gone down. Another solution is to use solar in **hybrid** systems. These combine solar with another source of energy, such as wind. The sun shines only during the day, but wind is stronger at night. Wind also increases during winter, when solar energy is less powerful. If they are used together, they can balance each other out.

Solar energy doesn't use fossil fuels that pollute the air, soil, and water. However, manufacturing PV solar cells does require toxic chemicals, which must be disposed of properly. Another problem with solar panels

is that they are clean freaks, and the world's a dirty place. Dust, snow, bird droppings, leaves, and other things can pile up on the surface of the panels. Even if only a small surface area is **obscured**, it can dramatically affect the efficiency of the panels. Maintenance crews have to keep the panels clean, but the never-ending job gets expensive.

Sunlight itself is free. It provides plenty of power, it's predictable, and it's available everywhere in the world. The technology to harness it appropriately is improving, and the costs are dropping. Even more important, governments are eager to find clean, secure sources of power. Solar power still provides less than 1 percent of the world's energy needs, but as long as the sun continues to shine, solar energy usage could grow even more.

Hybrid energy systems are more reliable than ones dependent on a single source.

CHAPTER THREE

A RAY OF HOPE

A CAT WILL LOOK FOR A SUNNY, WARM SPOT IN THE HOUSE TO GO TO SLEEP. People aren't quite so obvious about it, but a lot of them do basically the same thing. About 70 percent of the world's 7 billion people live in warm climates. It's expected that the global population will grow to about 9 billion by 2050. By then, about 80 percent of them will be huddled in the hot zones.

This is good news for solar power. While it probably can't solve the world's energy issues in the near future, such a heat-seeking

Warm-climate destinations, such as Miami, experience population growth during winter months.

trend suggests that the world's strongest solar resources—in deserts and near the equator—will be conveniently located near most of the world's people. Wherever people turn, there is plenty of sun. In the U.S., a field of solar panels in the Mojave Desert could supply enough electricity to power the whole country. The Chinese could use the Gobi Desert. The Sahara is perfect for Africa and Europe. Australia also has huge expanses of desert and sun. The continent is too far away from most places to directly export electricity, but the power could be used for electrolysis, the separation of water into hydrogen and oxygen. The hydrogen could then be exported for fuel.

In 2009, a group of European companies banded together to raise $555 billion to build commercial-sized CSP plants in Africa's Sahara Desert. The project was the brainchild of Dr. Gerhard Knies, a German physicist. He said, "We could meet the entire world's energy needs by covering a fraction of the world's deserts—just 0.5 percent—with concentrated solar power plants." In the U.S., four new CSP stations are planned for California and Nevada. They are scheduled to go online in 2016 and 2017. These

BrightSource's Ivanpah Solar Electric Generating System in the Mojave Desert will power 140,000 homes.

stations, as well as the African plant, would use thermal storage to save the sun's heat for times when the sun isn't shining.

With plenty of sunny deserts, why isn't solar being used everywhere? One problem is location. Electricity isn't a good traveler, and most large cities aren't in the middle of a desert. Electricity comes in two varieties: direct current and alternating current. Most households use alternating current. However, alternating current loses much of its power when it's moved over long distances. Some future transmission lines may use high-voltage direct current (HVDC) to get around the problem. HVDC is like an express train: it's well suited to moving electricity fast, over long distances, as long as there are no layovers.

Worldwide, industry experts say that the amount of PV solar power could grow to roughly 500 gigawatts by 2020. Much of that increase could be in areas that have good solar resources but limited (or no) access to grid-connected electricity. Several countries have set targets to increase the amount of solar power they generate. China is aiming for 20 gigawatts by 2015, and India wants the same amount by 2020. Algeria is working toward 10 gigawatts by 2030. Saudi Arabia is raising money for a $109-billion solar project that would provide a third of the nation's electricity by 2032.

In recent years, the price of PV panels has dropped dramatically, making it more popular than CSP in many places. These two technologies were formerly seen as competitors. However, developers are now looking into projects that combine both approaches. It's also possible that more power plants will

Solar panels are used around the world, from rooftops in China (left) to remote villages in India (below).

use some solar energy, even if they don't rely on it entirely. Developing countries, such as India and China, have a huge demand for electricity, and will probably continue to build new fossil fuel plants in the next few decades. However, they might be more environmentally friendly if they can at least be combined with solar technology. Solar energy could be used to preheat water before it enters a boiler at a conventional power plant, for example. More advanced systems could use solar power to boost output during times of heavy demand—and solar could even take over at times.

Improvements in storing energy will also make solar more **viable**. Thermal storage at CSP plants is one option. Another common way to store energy is in batteries. However, batteries are not particularly economical. They make sense for a flashlight in case the power goes out, but they cost a lot for the amount of energy they store. Also, to stash all the energy produced by solar electricity, a battery would have to be huge! There's progress being made on the energy storage front, though. Researchers in the U.S. are working on a liquid metal battery they believe will be ideal

Spain's Andasol 3 power plant uses a thermal storage system, allowing it to produce energy at night.

Batteries provide backup electricity for the renewably powered Scottish Isle of Eigg.

for storing excess energy from solar or wind power. It holds a lot of energy for its size, lasts a long time, and is relatively inexpensive.

Sunlight can't always penetrate Earth's atmosphere, so some scientists have proposed going the extra mile—or 22,400 miles (36,000 km), to be more precise. They want to put solar fields into Earth's orbit, where clouds or air pollution won't block the sun's rays. The solar collectors would use microwaves to beam the energy back to Earth. In 2009, a California solar company signed a contract with one of the state's utility companies to build such a system. Their plan called for it to be operational in 2016. Other space-based solar technologies could put

satellites closer to Earth, and long cables could be used to carry the electricity back down.

Other strides in solar technology are being made within the field of nanotechnology. This is the science of building things at the molecular level. A nanoparticle measures only one-billionth of a meter across. Fortunately, it doesn't require armies of elves with tweezers to link nanoparticles together. One of the astonishing characteristics of nanoparticles is that they can put themselves together. Nanoparticles can boost the efficiency of traditional PV cells because they allow the cells to absorb more light, which can then be converted into solar power. Scientists in

Using a microscope, an engineer in Chemnitz, Germany, examines a paper solar cell containing special ink.

the U.S. and Sweden are working on a kind of ink that contains nanoparticles. It can be printed on all kinds of surfaces—from the roofs of cars to the windows of homes. Because it's sprayed onto surfaces, rather than directly applied, it does not break delicate solar cells. It could even go onto thin, flexible solar cells embedded in the sleeve of a jacket. By carrying his own solar-powered portable charger, the wearer's cell phone might never say "Low Battery" again.

Light travels in waves. These waves come in different lengths that correspond to different colors. Most current PV cells do not recognize all of the different colors. Infrared light passes right through the cells, invisible to the electrons. Blue light is reflected back into the atmosphere. As a result, PV cells can use only a small segment of the light spectrum, reducing their efficiency. But some developers are working on what they call "multijunction" cells. These cells are treated with special dyes or chemicals that

NASA's Mars Exploration Rovers run the risk of becoming stranded if dust covers their solar panels.

allow them to capture red and blue light, boosting their efficiency to around 40 percent. Multijunction cells, which are used on spacecraft such as the Mars rovers, need direct, unscattered sunlight, so sophisticated tracking systems must keep them constantly pointed at the sun. Despite their small size, they take up a lot of room in a budget. They cost approximately $500 per square centimeter—though the cost is dropping.

The term "soft energy" describes energy that is renewable, flexible, and well suited to its environment and users. Solar energy as well as some forms of hydropower and wind power fall into this category. Today, people depend on centralized fossil fuel plants that distribute power through huge grids. In the future, some experts predict that people will use more locally produced energy. Additionally, instead of relying on a single energy type, people will be able to mix and match according to what makes sense for their environment. In such a scenario, solar could play a bigger role than ever.

CHAPTER FOUR

A ROOFTOP REVOLUTION

ACCORDING TO AN ANCIENT GREEK MYTH, A MAN
NAMED ICARUS USED A PAIR OF WAX WINGS TO
ESCAPE FROM A MAZE WHERE HE WAS IMPRISONED.
Icarus's father warned his son not to fly too close to the sun, or else
the wings would melt. Icarus ignored the advice, however, and fell
to his death. Some people believe that solar energy is not a good
solution for the world's energy needs because, like wax wings, it
cannot survive in the "heat" of the current energy market. Indeed,
within the last several years, the industry has taken a beating.
Many manufacturers have gone out of business as the competition
has stiffened. However, some experts argue that these are normal
"growing pains" to be expected as the industry matures.

With the industry still relatively young and small, it's not clear whether solar technology can make a dent in the world's energy needs. Proponents say that solar cells are getting better and cheaper all the time. Doubters argue that solar has too many problems, and that even miles of panels won't be enough to feed the world's demand for electricity. There are also concerns that solar's "green" image is not entirely accurate. Because solar power is intermittent, fossil fuel plants must make up the difference. Producing sudden bursts of power takes more energy than keeping a plant running at a constant pace. As a result, more **greenhouse gases** and pollutants are released. In addition, the process used to manufacture solar energy also releases greenhouse gases. The toxic chemicals used to produce PV cells stay in the environment for hundreds of years, so another problem that arises involves disposing of old solar panels. The average solar panel can last for 25 to 30 years. While there may not be much used equipment yet, people are concerned about this becoming a major problem in future decades.

A potential downside to widespread implementation of solar technology is how much space it requires. For people who think deserts are barren wastelands, it seems like an ideal use of the land to take it over with solar panels. However, it's controversial

Solar fields often take up thousands of acres of valuable agricultural land and wildlife habitat.

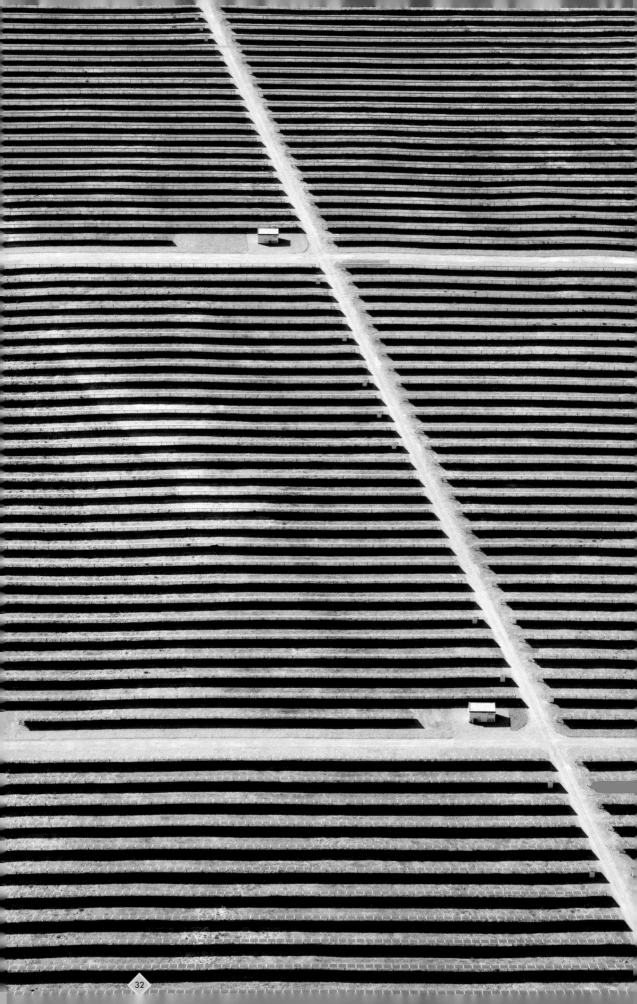

among environmentalists who want to protect the plant and animal species who thrive in desert habitats. They could be displaced by acres of solar farms.

So why not take advantage of all those rooftops? One problem with a "rooftop revolution" is that it requires rooftops. It's not difficult to put solar panels on large, suburban homes. But single-family homes are not the most energy-efficient way to live. Several large apartment buildings in jam-packed cities such as New York, Tokyo, or Calcutta have far less rooftop space than a single subdivision outside Minneapolis. But a lot more people live in apartments, so they use less energy per person. Rooftop solar works best on structures that are the least energy-efficient overall.

In addition, the efficiency of a solar system decreases at each stage of the manufacturing process. A solar cell may achieve 20 percent efficiency in a test environment. Manufacturing those cells in large amounts can drag the efficiency down a few points. Add in wear and tear once the panels are being used in the real

Photovoltaic power plants are often called solar farms or parks, as in Bulgaria (left) and Shanghai, China (below).

world, and the power output drops farther. Also, transforming electricity into alternating current for household use reduces its overall efficiency. Finally, even though the photovoltaic part of a cell can last for decades, the electrical wiring fails much sooner, lasting only five to eight years.

Probably the biggest drawback to solar is its cost. Historically, solar has been significantly more expensive than fossil fuels, nuclear power, or even other renewables such as wind power. The price has dropped significantly in recent years, mostly thanks to improvements in manufacturing and distribution. However, there are unknowns about how durable solar systems are and how long they will last.

Nonetheless, most nations today are working to make renewable energy a bigger part of their energy mix—and the faster, the better. One reason is "energy security." Many nations want the independence that comes from supplying their own sources of energy, and not relying on importing it from other countries. One advantage to **domestic** sources of energy is that there are lower transportation costs, which makes it less expensive. In addition, a nation does not have to bargain with other countries to buy fuel. That stabilizes the prices, and reduces the risk of losing the supply altogether if political relations become hostile.

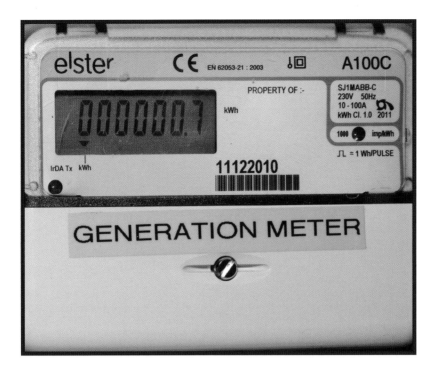

In Barcelona, Spain, solar panels became exterior walls (left). A FIT system uses a meter to record how much electricity solar panels generate (above).

In many countries, the solar industry has been helped by a financial incentive called a feed-in tariff (FIT). This guarantees that producers will have a market for the energy they produce and that they will be paid a certain amount of money for the power they "feed in" to the electrical grid. In the late 1980s, feed-in tariffs began in Germany, which helped the solar market grow there. Some critics disapproved of Germany's extensive **subsidies**, arguing that the costs were greater than the return. However, the subsidies have helped new companies fine-tune their manufacturing processes and reduce costs, which could provide more long-term benefits. As solar technology has improved and costs have dropped, governments have scaled back how much money they kick in. As a whole, the industry is listening to a ticking clock. Governments are not likely to support renewables such as solar and wind energy with subsidies forever. These industries will have to sink or swim on their own. In fact, the IEA estimates that the renewable energy industry will grow more as a result of a **carbon tax** on fossil fuels than on subsidies awarded by governments.

New business models may become part of the equation, too. Instead of selling a homeowner a solar system outright, which can cost about $20,000, some companies lease the equipment to customers for a monthly fee. The cost is offset by the savings on a typical electric bill. In the African country of Kenya, the British solar technology company Eight19 installs low-cost solar power units in people's homes. Customers use it only when they need it. They buy a scratch card which has a code that they text to the company to activate the unit. Over time, they can buy the unit.

Solar could also benefit from a new way of distributing electricity. A "smart grid" could automatically dispense electricity during times of low demand, especially for tasks that are not time-sensitive (such as running the dishwasher). In addition, if a small-scale solar system used by an individual or community makes extra electricity, that energy could be sold back to the grid for someone else to use. It would be the ultimate "extra credit"!

Danny Kennedy is the head of the California solar company Sungevity and a longtime advocate of solar power. In a 2012 interview with the *New York Times*, he pointed out, "We [drill for gas in] our own backyards and pollute our rivers, or we blow up our mountaintops ... for an hour of electricity, when we could just take what's falling free from the sky.... Humanity needs to be reminded that the sun's putting out four hundred trillion trillion watts every second of every day, and we should tap that."

Throughout history, people have questioned the need for new technologies—such as cars and telephones—that ended up becoming commonplace. The same might be said for solar energy. Today, solar provides only a tiny amount of the world's energy needs. It doesn't have enough momentum to take over the world next year or even for several years. But like the sun, it's a rising star. There's nowhere to go but up.

According to the IEA, solar energy has the potential to provide one-third of the world's energy by 2060.

Mounted on a giant cart, Antoine Lavoisier's "burning lens" was probably an intimidating sight in 1774. The French chemist had constructed a lens made of two pieces of glass, four feet (1.2 m) in diameter, which he used to focus the sun's rays. Reaching temperatures of 3,000 °F (1,649 °C), the solar furnace could melt chemicals and metal. Lavoisier's other experiments led to his suggesting the existence of silicon, an element used to make photovoltaic solar panels today. Unfortunately, Lavoisier's scientific research was cut short when he was executed in 1794, during the French Revolution (1787–99).

By the mid-1800s, several solar gadgets had been invented, but French teacher and inventor Augustin Mouchot wasn't satisfied. He wanted to use solar energy for more practical purposes. Steam engines were the dominant machines of the time, but they used mostly coal. Mouchot set out to design a solar-powered steam engine, reaching his goal in 1866. Mouchot also conducted experiments in which he used solar power for the electrolysis of water, the process of passing an electrical current through water to separate it into its two elemental parts, hydrogen and oxygen. The hydrogen could then be used to create electricity.

The "father of modern chemistry," Antoine Lavoisier (left) is known for his influential work with oxygen and combustion and for discovering the law of conservation of mass.

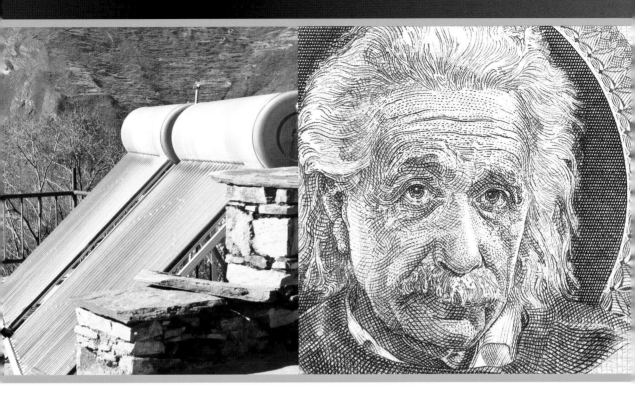

Clarence Kemp wanted to help his fellow man. When his neighbors' wives left for an extended summer vacation, the men had to perform the household chores themselves. In 1891, having enough hot water was a constant battle. While simple metal water tanks absorbed some heat, they weren't efficient. And heating water on the stove was no fun during a hot and humid summer in Maryland, where Kemp lived. Kemp invented a solar water heater that used the idea of a "hot box." The tanks were surrounded by glass that insulated and retained the heat. The "Climax" was an instant hit.

Throughout the 1800s, scientists had observed that when light interacted with other substances, it sometimes could create electricity. But how, exactly, did it work? In 1905, the famous German-American physicist Albert Einstein published a paper that helped explain the process. He proposed that light was not simply a wave, but was made up of a group of particles, later called photons. When substances absorbed the photons, it would agitate their electrons, causing them to move around and produce an electric current. Einstein's discovery of the law of the photoelectric effect helped him earn the Nobel Prize in 1921.

Homes in developing parts of the world such as Tibet utilize rooftop solar systems (center) to heat water. Albert Einstein's (right) work with photons was crucial to quantum theory.

After the first practical solar cell was demonstrated in 1954, the question became what to do with it. Dr. Hans Ziegler, who worked for the U.S. Army Signal Corps, had an idea. The navy was building a satellite to be launched into space. They wanted to use batteries to power the onboard equipment, but Ziegler believed that lightweight solar cells, combined with their renewable power source, would work better. In 1958, *Vanguard I* became the first spacecraft to use solar power. Ziegler was proven correct: *Vanguard's* regular battery died after less than three weeks, but the solar cells lasted seven years.

Could solar energy really be used to generate electricity on a large scale? The U.S. government decided to find out. In 1982, a project called Solar One was the first "utility-sized" attempt at concentrated solar power (CSP). Built in California's Mojave Desert, this "power tower" used thousands of heliostats (mirrors) to focus and collect solar heat. Solar One shut down in 1986 but was revived in 1995 as Solar Two. This time, the plant used molten salt, instead of water and oil, to transfer heat. This allowed energy to be stored for longer periods of time. Solar Two closed in 1999.

Although deserts seem ideal places for collecting solar energy, drawbacks such as dust, lack of water for cooling, and environmental concerns have made progress slow.

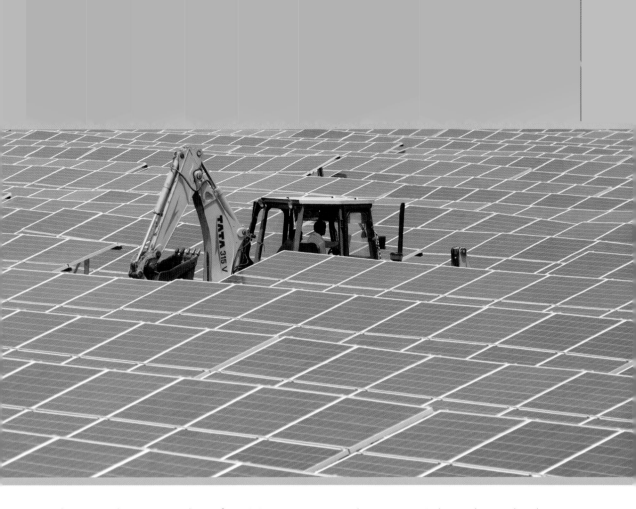

For three weeks in December of 1982 and January of 1983 the sun beat down on Hans Tholstrup and Larry Perkins as they drove across the Australian outback. That was just what they wanted, since their car depended entirely on solar power. Tholstrup designed the car because he was interested in using renewable energy sources. "The Quiet Achiever" was a strange sight: it looked like a small boat with a flat, white top. But it worked: it traveled 2,500 miles (4,000 km) on nothing but the sun. The journey led to Tholstrup's starting the World Solar Challenge, a competition for solar cars, in 1987.

The Gujarat Solar Park in India doesn't have any rides, but the theme is pretty clear: sun, sun, and more sun. Construction began in 2010 on this group of solar farms, which are run by different companies but share a common infrastructure. Taken together, they make Gujarat the largest photovoltaic power station in the world. About 856 megawatts of capacity were installed by March 2013, with 1,000 megawatts projected by the end of 2013. India has a goal of producing 20 gigawatts of solar power by 2020.

An excavator works among the PV solar panels at India's Gujarat Solar Park (above). The park is expected to save millions of tons of carbon dioxide emissions each year.

GLOSSARY

atom—the smallest possible unit of a chemical element

carbon tax—a fee that companies who produce large amounts of pollutants must pay

deity—a god

domestic—within any given nation; not involving other countries

electron—a negatively charged particle located within an atom

fossil fuels—fuels formed by decaying plants and animals over millions of years

global warming—the phenomenon of Earth's average temperatures increasing over time

greenhouse gas—a gas that builds up in Earth's atmosphere and prevents the release of heat

hybrid—a combination of two or more things, used to complement one another

infrastructure—the services and mechanisms used to support a society

intermittent—occurring occasionally and often unpredictably

molten—in a liquid state, melted

obscured—blocked, unable to be seen

parabolic—shaped like a bowl

piston—a moving part in an engine that delivers force

power grid—a system for distributing power throughout a community

renewable—able to be replenished and used indefinitely

subsidies—money supplied by a government to help pay for something

turbine—a machine that is driven by water, steam, or a gas flowing through the blades of a wheel

viable—capable of being successful

SELECTED BIBLIOGRAPHY

Butti, Ken, and John Perlin. *A Golden Thread*. New York: Van Nostrand Reinhold, 1980.

Chiras, Dan. *Solar Electricity Basics: A Green Energy Guide*. Gabriola Island, B.C.: New Society Publishers, 2010.

DeGunther, Rik. *Alternative Energy for Dummies*. Hoboken, N.J.: Wiley, 2009.

Economist.com. "A Painful Eclipse." October 15, 2011.

Himmelman, Jeff. "The Secret to Solar Power." *New York Times Magazine*, August 9, 2012.

International Energy Agency. *Solar Energy Perspectives*. Paris: Organization for Economic Cooperation and Development, 2011.

Wald, Matthew L. "Storehouses for Solar Energy Can Step in When the Sun Goes Down." *New York Times*, January 2, 2012.

Zehner, Ozzie. *Green Illusions: The Dirty Secrets of Clean Energy and the Future of Environmentalism*. Lincoln: University of Nebraska Press, 2012.

Going Green Challenge

http://www.going-green-challenge.com/solar-energy-for-kids.html
This site offers an overview of solar energy, a timeline of its history, prospects for the future, and links to do-it-yourself solar projects.

Solar Energy International

http://www.solarenergy.org/answers-older-kids
Solar Energy International, a nonprofit organization dedicated to solar research, answers questions about how solar power works and its various uses.

NOTE: *Every effort has been made to ensure that the websites listed above are suitable for children, that they have educational value, and that they contain no inappropriate material. However, because of the nature of the Internet, it is impossible to guarantee that these sites will remain active indefinitely or that their contents will not be altered.*

Dorion, Christiane. *Are We Running out of Energy?* Mankato, Minn.: Arcturus, 2008.

Gunderson, Jessica. *The Energy Dilemma*. Mankato, Minn.: Creative Education, 2011.

Morris, Neil. *The Energy Mix*. Mankato, Minn.: Smart Apple Media, 2010.

—————. *Solar Power*. Mankato, Minn.: Smart Apple Media, 2010.

Oxlade, Chris. *Energy Technology*. Mankato, Minn.: Smart Apple Media, 2012.

Royston, Angela. *Sustainable Energy*. Mankato, Minn.: Arcturus, 2009.

Solway, Andrew. *Climate Change*. Mankato, Minn.: Smart Apple Media, 2010.

HARNESSING ENERGY • HARNESSING ENERGY •

Published by Creative Paperbacks
P.O. Box 227, Mankato, Minnesota 56002
Creative Paperbacks is an imprint of The Creative Company
www.thecreativecompany.us

Design and production by The Design Lab
Art direction by Rita Marshall
Printed in the United States of America

Photographs by Alamy (Eye Ubiquitous, INTERFOTO, PBstock, Jim West), Corbis
(AMIT DAVE/Reuters, Bettmann, Ashley Cooper, MIGUEL ANGEL MOLINA/
epa, Proehl Studios, Bob Sacha, Hendrik Schmidt/dpa, George Steinmetz, Jim
West/imagebroker), Dreamstime (Airwolf01, Piero Cruciatti, Kvisitsopa, Zuzana
Randlova, Samrat35, Tangencial, Michael Wood), NASA (NASA/jpl/nasa.gov),
Shutterstock (anyaivanova, ArchMan, ArtisticPhoto, Sissy Borbely, Richard Cavalleri,
Matteo Festi, Georgios Kollidas, lumen-digital, Arkady Mazor, mikeledray, Dudarev
Mikhail, Gencho Petkov, pixinoo, Portokalis, Joshua Resnick, Vadim Sadovski)

Library of Congress Cataloging-in-Publication Data
Bailey, Diane.
Solar power / Diane Bailey.
p. cm. — (Harnessing energy)
Includes bibliographical references and index.
Summary: An examination of the ways in which the sun has historically
been used as an energy source and how current and future energy
demands are changing its technical applications and efficiency levels.
ISBN 978-1-60818-412-5 (hardcover)
ISBN 978-0-89812-998-4 (pbk)
1. Photovoltaic power generation—Juvenile literature.
2. Solar energy—Juvenile literature. I. Title.

TK1087.B335 2014
621.47—dc23   2013035756

CCSS: RI.5.1, 2, 3, 4, 8, 9

First Edition
9 8 7 6 5 4 3 2 1